WHAT

IS

BORN

AGAIN

????

Frank Edward Cassidy

In Memory of
Barbara Walton (Coffin) Cassidy
1923-1994

Contents

PREFACE

To be born again is the essence of Christianity. This book gives
the fundamental steps to becoming a Christian. I have written
it as simply as possible for the reader to understand. I have been
brief so the reader can quickly read through and grasp the contents.
But, I was not so brief as not to cover the subject sufficiently.

Jesus said, "Go therefore and make disciples of all the nations,"
(Matthew 28:19). The word disciple literally means "a learner." To
make someone a disciple means to teach. The Great Commission is
to teach the nations about Jesus and to bring them into the kingdom
of God. This book was written to teach. First, to teach Christians
what being Born Again is all about. Second, so Christians can disciple (teach) others about Jesus. Third, this book is intended for the
unbeliever to be able to read the text and understand: a.) Why one
must become Born Again, b.) What Born Again means, c.) How to
be Born Again, and finally, d.) When to be Born Again.

"What is Born Again" is written for readers of all ages. I believe
that the people of generation "X", those born after 1956, will gain
most from this book. Since 1963 Bible reading has not been a part
of the public school student's life in the United States. Many people
have never heard or read the Bible, nor have they attended Church.
Their knowledge about the Bible and Christianity comes from what
they have learned through the negative influences of TV,
Hollywood, and rock music.

In this work I do not attempt to prove that there is a God, but I begin with the premise that there is a God and the Bible is His uncompromising Word. If the reader does not believe in God, I suggest that he or she read C. S. Lewis' "Mere Christianity". Professor Lewis presents the best argument for the existence of the great God and Creator of heaven and earth.

The Bible quotes used are from the New American Standard Bible, Published by A. J. Holman Company, division of J. B. Lippincott Company, Philadelphia and New York. The other version of the Bible used is marked as follows:

N. I. V.   New International Version of the Holy Bible
                 Zondervan Bible Publishers
                 Grand Rapids, Michigan

I chose the New American Standard Bible because of its accuracy and my familiarity with this version. The New International Version is used because in some cases it is much clearer for the reader.

It is my desire and sincere belief that each reader will come to know the truth about being a Christian, being set free to enter into the kingdom of God for eternity, through the acceptance of Jesus the Christ as their Lord and Savior.

I wish to thank the many teachers I was privileged to sit under these many years. Their dedication and work influenced this book. There are too many to name, but a special, "thank you", goes to Dr. Bill Kaiser for his teaching of body, soul, and spirit. Most importantly I wish to thank my wife, Marilynn, for the many hours of work editing, her constant support and encouragement through many difficult times.

CHAPTER ONE

WHY SHOULD I BE BORN AGAIN?

Chuck Colson wrote a book in the 1970's called "Born Again". People began using the term almost everywhere. Football teams that made a comeback were said to be born again. The U. S. Presidents, Jimmy Carter and Ronald Regan, were said to be born again. But, why must we be Born Again? What is Born Again? How do we become Born Again? And, when should we become Born Again? Let's start with the "Why".

BEFORE THE CREATION OF MAN

To find the "Why", we will go back before the creation of man, to see who committed the first sin. We will look at how God dealt with the sinner. The first chapter of Genesis outlines the creation of the universe and the creation of man. The second chapter shows how God brought man into existence. Next are God's instructions to Adam. Later in chapter two we see God bringing woman into existence by a different means than He used for Adam. Genesis, chapter three, tells how man defected, causing the loss of his authority over the earth and the curse he came to live under.

"In the beginning God created the heavens and the earth" (Genesis 1:1). There is a theory that a gap exists between verses one and two. The "gap theory" claims something happened to stop the creation of the universe. Many centuries later God gives us a glimpse of the rebellion in a lamentation recorded by the prophet Ezekiel:

> 11) Again the word of the LORD came to me saying,
>
> 12) "Son of man, take up a lamentation over the king of Tyre, and say to him, 'thus says the Lord God, "You had the seal of perfection, full of wisdom and perfect in beauty.
>
> 13) "You were in Eden, the garden of God; every precious stone was your covering: the ruby, the topaz and the diamond; the beryl, the onyx, and the jasper; the lapis lazuli, the turquoise, and the emerald; and the gold, the workmanship of your settings and sockets, was in you. On the day that you were created they were prepared.
>
> 14) "You were the anointed cherub who covers, and I placed you there. You were on the holy mountain of God; you walked in the midst of the stones of fire.
>
> 15) "You were blameless in your ways from the day you were created, until unrighteousness was found in you.
>
> 16) "By the abundance of your trade you were internally filled with violence, and you sinned; therefore, I have cast you as profane from the mountain of God. And I have destroyed you, O covering cherub, from the midst of the stones of fire.
>
> 17) "Your heart was lifted up because of your beauty; you corrupted your wisdom by reason of your splendor. I cast you to the ground; I put you before kings, that they may see you.
>
> 18) "By the multitude of your iniquities, in the unrighteousness of your trade, you profaned your sanctuaries. Therefore I have brought fire from the

midst of you, it has consumed you, and I have turned
you to ashes on the earth in the eyes of all who see
you.

19) "All who know you among the peoples are
appalled at you; you have become terrified and you
will be no more." ' " (Ezekiel 28:11-19)

THE ONE CALLED SATAN

This passage of Scripture starts with God telling Ezekiel to
write ". . . a lamentation over the king of Tyre". We quickly realize
God is not talking about a man. Verses 14 and 16 use the term
"cherub", a type of angel. Also, in verse 14, God says: ". . . You
were on the holy mountain of God". Whom is God talking about?
He is speaking of the one called Satan or the Devil.

What happened to this "anointed cherub?" Ezekiel 28:16-18
shows that Satan was found unrighteous "by the abundance of your
trade . . . " [He was] "filled with violence . . ." [and he] "sinned . . ."
"Your heart was lifted up because of your beauty; you corrupted
your wisdom by reason of your splendor . . ." [and] "by the multi-
tude of your iniquities, in the unrighteousness of your trade, you
profaned your sanctuaries.". In other words, he became arrogant.
Looking at Ezekiel 28:11-19 we see four phases that Satan goes
through:

1) He was created in beauty and blameless.
2) He became proud and sinned.
3) He was cast down.
4) He will be no more.

Another reference to the fall of Satan is found in Isaiah 14:1-23.
Also, Jesus refers to the fall of Satan: "and He said of them, "I was
watching Satan fall from heaven like lightening."" (Luke 10:18).

Before Satan was banished from heaven, we believe heaven was
populated by God and the angels. After Satan's fall, one third of the
angels left with him. We see this in Revelation: "And his tail

[Satan's] swept away a third of the stars of heaven, and threw them to the earth" (Revelation 12:4a). The stars refer to the angels of heaven. Three Scriptures refer to "the angels of Satan, the devil, or the old serpent":

> "For if God did not spare angels when they sinned, but cast them into hell and committed them to pits of darkness, reserved for judgement. . ." (2 Peter 2:4)

> "And angels who did not keep their own domain, but abandoned their proper abode, He has kept in eternal bonds under darkness for the judgement of the great day." (Jude 6)

> "And the great dragon was thrown down, the serpent of old who is called the devil and Satan, who deceives the whole world; he was thrown down to the earth, and his angels were thrown down with him." (Revelation 12:9)

A great defection from heaven has taken place, and now a great void exists.

GOD CREATES MAN

One of two possible situations exists. The first is that God now plans to repopulate heaven with a new species, man. The other possibility is God had already decided to create man. But, in either case, God will not let heaven suffer the violence of sin again. God planned a test of loyalty to see if His new creation would obey Him. So He created man and placed him in a perfect environment for this test.

Looking again at Genesis, we see that God is planning, setting up authority for, and creating man:

> 26) Then God said, "Let Us make man in Our image, according to Our likeness, and let them rule

over the fish of the sea and over the birds of the sky
and over the cattle and over all the earth, and over
every creeping thing that creeps on the earth."

27) And God created man in His own image, in the
image of God He created him; male and female He
created them. (Genesis 1:26-27)

Man was created in God's image. In what respect is man made
in God's image? Since we do not know what God looks like, what
does "in His image" mean? We can understand this better when we
know that God is a spirit, an eternal living being: "God is spirit, and
those who worship Him must worship in spirit and truth." (John
4:24). This means that man must be a spirit being also. Now, obviously we see each other, but, we cannot see God. So, what makes us
different from God? We are also a physical being. We see this in
Genesis 2:7: "Then the LORD God formed man of dust from the
ground, and breathed into his nostrils the breath of life; and man
became a living being.".

THE THREE PART MAN

First, we can see that man's physical being was formed out of
the dust of the ground. Second, what did God breathe into Adam? If
God is a spirit, He must have breathed spirit into man. So spirit
must be the substance or foundation of life. Man became a "living
being". In Hebrew, "living" means a soul being. Another way to
interpret soul is mind. Adam was formed a physical being. Then
Adam had spirit breathed into him, making him a spiritual being,
and he became a soul being.

Looking more closely at man's three parts, we can break each
part into sub-parts. The body of man is made of flesh, blood, and
bone. The soul or mind of man is made up of emotions, will, and
intellect. The spirit of man is made up of communion, intuition, and
conscience.

Outlining this, we see:

COMMUNION

:

(SPIRIT)   **INTUITION**

:

CONSCIENCE

:

(SOUL)   **EMOTIONS   WILL   INTELLECT**

===

BONE

:

(BODY)   **BLOOD**

:

FLESH

It is important to remember this outline and particularly the place we see the "WILL". It is in dead-center.

IN THE GARDEN

In Genesis 2:9, God plants a garden for Adam. Two of the trees in the garden are different from the rest. One is "THE TREE OF LIFE", and the other is "THE TREE OF THE KNOWLEDGE OF GOOD AND EVIL". Verses 15-17 shows the consequences of eating from The Tree of the Knowledge of Good and Evil:

> 15) Then the LORD God took the man and put him into the garden of Eden to cultivate it and keep it.
> 16) And the LORD God commanded the man, saying, "From any tree of the garden you may eat freely;
> 17) but from the tree of the knowledge of good and evil you shall not eat, for in the day that you eat from it you shall surely die." (Genesis 2:15-17)

Man was given control of the garden with only one restriction, not to eat of "The Tree of the Knowledge of Good and Evil". He was told that he would die if he ate from it. A more literal translation of verse 17 is: "in the day you eat from it 'in dying' you shall surely die." This verse shows that a man faces two deaths. The two types of death are physical and spiritual. Physical death occurs when the spirit of man is separated from the physical body. Spiritual death is when the spirit of man is separated from God for eternity.

ADAM'S HELPER

Moving to verse 18: "Then the LORD God said, 'it is not good for man to be alone; I will make him a helper suitable for him'". In verses 19 and 20 we see God bringing the animals to Adam. Adam names each animal, but no suitable helper is found. Adam probably enjoyed the cats and dogs, he probably used the horses and elephants for work, but he must have still felt alone. God already had a plan. God used this time to get some work done, such as naming the animals, before He introduced the helper He had planned for Adam:

> 21) So the LORD God caused a deep sleep to fall upon the man, and he slept; them He took one of his ribs, and closed up the flesh at that place.
> 22) And the LORD God fashioned into a woman the rib which He had taken from the man, and brought her to the man.
> 23) And the man said, "This is now bone of my bones, and flesh of my flesh; She shall be called Woman, because she was taken out of man."
> 24) For this cause a man shall leave his father and mother, and shall cleave to his wife, and they shall become one flesh.
> 25) And the man and his wife were both naked and were not ashamed. (Genesis 2:21-25)

Now creation is complete. Adam has his helper, the animals

have names and all is well.

Interestingly, God used a rib to form woman. Someone once said: "God used a rib, because if He took a bone from Adam's foot, man would walk over woman. If God took a bone from Adam's head, woman would be over man. But God used a rib from under his arm to protect her, and next to his heart to love her." Now God had made man; "...He created him; male and female He created them." (Genesis 1:27b).

DECEPTION AND DISOBEDIENCE

The third chapter of Genesis takes us into a day in the life of the man and woman. We have no idea how long it has been since the end of chapter two. We do not know if it has been days, weeks, months, or even years.

> 1) Now the serpent was more crafty than any beast of the field which the LORD God made. And he said to the woman, "Indeed, has God said, 'you shall not eat from any tree of the garden'?"
> 2) And the woman said to the serpent, "from the fruit of the trees of the garden we may eat;
> 3) but from the fruit of the tree which is in the middle of the garden, God has said, 'you shall not eat from it or touch it, lest you die.'"
> 4) And the serpent said to the woman, "You surely shall not die!
> 5) For God knows that in the day you eat from it your eyes will be opened, and you will be like God, knowing good and evil."
> 6) When the woman saw that the tree was good for food, and that it was a delight to the eyes and that the tree was desirable to make one wise, she took from its fruit and ate; and she gave also to her husband with her, and he ate.
> 7) then the eyes of both of them were opened, and they knew they were naked; and they sewed fig

leaves together and made themselves loin coverings.
(Genesis 3:1-7)

Genesis chapter three starts with a conversation between the serpent and the woman. In this day and age the thought of an animal talking is strange. First we must remember that the third chapter shows a major change in the world. Talking animals may have been commonplace before this. Or, the serpent may have been able to speak because it was possessed by a spirit being, Satan. The conversation was obviously not the first. The woman was not alarmed by the serpent or by the fact that he talked. Also, the woman trusted what the serpent said; possibly they had many conversations before this event. Slowly the serpent had built up the woman's confidence in him, so at this point the woman readily took the serpent at his word.

The woman did not have a good understanding of God's command in reference to the tree. In verse three she says: ". . . you shall not eat from it or touch it" (Genesis 3:3). Nowhere do we see that there was a command to "not touch the tree". This is probably because the information is second hand from Adam, or he gave her incorrect information. Verse six shows that she sees the tree: ". . . was good for food, . . . a delight to the eye". [and it] ". . . was desirable to make one wise" (Genesis 3:6). Human nature has an unquenchable thirst for knowledge. Our libraries, universities, research laboratories, and news programs all feed our desire for knowledge. Here Eve is tempted with the possibility of gaining knowledge, knowledge equal to God's. She saw that the fruit was visually delightful, and: ". . . made one wise" (Genesis 3:6). These factors drew her into taking and eating the fruit. In other words, the serpent beguiled her with his craftiness.

Now Adam is not left out of the picture. We see in verse six: ". . . and she gave also to her husband with her" (Genesis 3:6). Adam was with her. We do not know if he heard the conversation, but he was close enough to see her take the fruit. And verse six ends with: ". . . and he ate.". Why did Adam eat? God had told Adam, not to eat of the tree! Was he also beguiled by the serpent's words? Had he forgotten the instructions? Adam saw the woman eat and nothing happened to her. Adam may have asked himself, "Why did she not drop dead on the spot?"

THE CONSEQUENCES OF DISOBEDIENCE

The rest of Genesis chapter 3 shows the immediate effect of man's disobedience.

> 8) And they heard the sound of the LORD God walking in the garden in the cool of the day, and the man and his wife hid themselves from the presence of the LORD God among the trees of the garden.
> 9) The LORD God called to the man, and said to him, "Where are you?"
> 10) And he said, "I heard the sound of Thee in the garden, and I was
> afraid because I was naked; so I hid myself."
> 11) And He said, "who told you that you were naked? Have you eaten from the tree of which I commanded you not to eat?
> 12) And the man said, "the woman whom Thou gavest to be with me, she gave me from the tree, and I ate."
> 13) Then the LORD God said to the woman, "What is this you have done?" And the woman said, "The serpent deceived me, and I ate."
> 14 And the LORD God said to the serpent, "Because you have done this, cursed are you more than all cattle, and more than every beast of the field;
>
> > On your belly you shall go,
> > And dust shall you eat
> > All the days of your life. (Genesis 3:8-14)

Verses eight through 14 show a dialogue between the LORD God, the man, and the woman. We see the first "buck-passer" when Adam says: "...The woman whom Thou gavest to be with me, she gave me from the tree, and I ate". The woman was a little smarter: '...And the woman said, "The serpent . . . deceived me, and I ate'". Neither the man nor the woman would directly say: "I have made a mistake, please forgive me". Then God put a curse on an animal because of his part.

Next, God makes a prophetic statement that will set the course of history:

> And I will put enmity
> Between you and the woman
> And between your seed and her seed;
> He shall bruise you on the head,
> and you shall bruise him on the heel." (Genesis 3:15)

In verse 15 God is still talking to the serpent, who represents Satan. The enmity is the struggle between man, represented as the seed of the woman, and the power of the evil one. Satan's constant effort is to lead man down the path of destruction, keeping him away from God and the future blessing of eternity in heaven. We must remember the Bible is written in a middle Eastern cultural setting. The reference of "bruising the head" symbolizes the loss of a ruler's power. Power is transferred to the one who bruises the head. The bruising of the heel is the prophesy of God's plan for man's salvation:

> 16) To the woman He said, "I will greatly multiply your pain in childbirth, in pain you shall bring forth children; yet your desire shall be for your husband, and he shall rule over you."
> 17) Then to Adam He said, 'because you have listened to the voice of your wife, and have eaten from the tree about which I commanded you, saying, 'you shall not eat from it'; cursed is the ground because of you; in toil you shall eat of it all the days of your life.
> 18) "Both thorns and thistles it shall grow for you; and you shall eat the plants of the field;
> 19) By the sweat of your face you shall eat bread, till

you return to the ground, because from it you were taken; for you are dust, And to dust you shall return." (Genesis 3:16-19)

In verses 16-19, God tells the woman and man the consequence of their disobedience in eating of the Tree of the Knowledge of Good and Evil.

A MAJOR CHANGE

There has been a major change in the world of the man and the woman. Adam begins calling the woman Eve: "Now the man called his wife's name Eve, because she was the mother of all living." (Genesis 3:20). In verse 21 the first blood is shed when God makes Adam and Eve clothing from the skins of animals. "And the LORD God made garments of skin for Adam and his wife, and clothed them.". In verses 22-24 Adam and Eve are driven out of the garden:

22) The LORD God said, "Behold, the man has become like one of Us, knowing good and evil; and now, lest he stretch out his hand, and take also from the tree of life, and eat, and live forever"-
23) therefore the LORD God sent him out from the garden of Eden, to cultivate the ground from which he was taken.
24) So He drove the man out; and at the east of the garden of Eden He stationed the cherubim, and the flaming sword which turned every direction, to guard the way to the tree of life. (Genesis 3:22-24)

DRIVEN FROM THE GARDEN

Interestingly the twenty-second verse ends as though God stopped talking in the middle of the sentence. Possibly God decided He must act before the man and woman could eat from the "Tree of Life". This would leave man in an even worse state. Man would degenerate deeper into evil with no way out. We can see throughout the book of Genesis that man became so depraved that God had to wipe all, but Noah and his family, off the face of the earth. To emphasize the importance of man not eating of the "Tree of Life", He stationed angels to keep man from the "Tree of Life". If man had first eaten from the "Tree fo Life" how different his life would have been. God would have had to keep man from the Tree of the "Knowledge of Good and Evil" to protect man from living eternally in an unredeemable state of evil.

THE SECOND TEST

God's testing has begun and the first round went to Satan. But God's plan is still to test man to see if man will be loyal. So God goes to plan "B", so to speak, when He says:

> And I will put enmity
> Between you and the woman,
> And between your seed and her seed; He shall bruise
> you on the head, And you shall bruise him on the
> heel." (Genesis 3:15)

God's plan is to raise up a champion to take back the authority man has lost, and to give man an avenue to regain his proper place with God. We see several references to this testing in this psalm of king David:

PSALM 1

> 1) How blessed is the man who does not walk in the counsel of the wicked, Nor stand in the path of sinners, Nor sit in the seat of scoffers!
> 2) But his delight is in the law of the LORD, And in His law he meditates day and night.
> 3) And he will be like a tree firmly planted by streams of water,
> Which yields its fruit in its season,

And its leaf does not wither;
And in whatever he does, he prospers.
4) The wicked are not so, but they are like chaff
which the wind drives away.
5) Therefore the wicked will not stand in the judgement, nor sinners in the assembly of the righteous.
6) For the LORD knows the way of the righteous.
But the way of the wicked will perish.

Note the use of the word "chaff", the unused part of the wheat. We see this again: "Therefore, they will be like the morning cloud, and like dew which soon disappears, like chaff which is blown away from the threshing floor, and like smoke from a chimney." (Hosea. 13:3). John the Baptist put it best this way: "And His winnowing fork is in His hand, and He will thoroughly clear His threshing floor; and He will gather His wheat into the barn, but He will burn up the chaff with unquenchable fire." (Matthew 3:12). Interestingly, John uses the word "winnowing fork" and "threshing floor" to describe the testing of man. After the testing, the wheat, who are the obedient, will be gathered into the barn, which is heaven. The chaff, the disobedient, will be sent to eternal destruction.

Looking again at the outline of the three part man:

COMMUNION

:

(SPIRIT)   **INTUITION**

:

CONSCIENCE

:

(SOUL)   **EMOTIONS   WILL   INTELLECT**

BONE

:

(BODY)   **BLOOD**

:

FLESH

We see that <u>WILL</u> is in the middle. God created man with a will to decide whether he would be faithful to God or not. The test God set up was very simple. All Adam had to do was not eat of "The Tree of the Knowledge of Good and Evil". Adam is given the right to choose to obey God or not.

Adam, for whatever reason, decided to eat of "The Tree of the Knowledge of Good and Evil". Now it is interesting to note that the woman ate of the tree and nothing happened. This leads us to believe that it is not the tree that is the source of sin but the willful act of Adam that caused sin to enter the earth. Genesis 3:6 ends with: ". . . and he ate". Verse seven continues, "Then the eyes of both of them were opened". "Therefore, just as 'through one man sin entered into the world, and death through sin, and so death spread to all men, because all sinned -" (Romans 5:12). Not until after Adam ate were their eyes opened.

From this time on, all men were born into sin. The apostle Paul in his letter to the church at Rome said: "For all have sinned and fall short of the glory of God," (Romans 3:23). Adam was the surrogate, the representative of all mankind. Adam's failure shows that man would need help to be permitted into heaven.

CHAPTER TWO

WHAT IS BORN AGAIN?

What does "Born Again" mean, and where does it originate? There are only two places in the Bible where the term "Born Again" can be found. The first is in the book of John chapter 3:3&7. These verses relate to a conversation between Nicodemus, a member of the ruling Sanhedrin, and Jesus. The second place "Born Again" is found is in I Peter 1:23, and it echoes the first reference because Peter was with John at the original meeting.

A SECRET FOLLOWER

First let us set the stage for the conversation between Nicodemus and Jesus. Nicodemus was a member of a religious sect, called Pharisees, founded about 300 years before the birth of Jesus. Pharisees were part of the Jewish ruling body called the Sanhedrin. Although Israel was under the control of Rome, Israel maintained an independent religious ruling body. The leader of the Sanhedrin was the High Priest of the Temple. This body had seventy members, as in the days of Moses, made up of: Priests, Pharisees, Sadducees, and Scribes. The function of the Sanhedrin was to administer the Mosaic law. It worked much like the Supreme Court of the United States.

Nicodemus was a Pharisee, a teacher of the law. The Pharisees were strict interpreters of the Mosaic law. They had developed an unwritten law known as the "Traditional Law". One of the reasons why they wanted to kill Jesus was because of His condemnation of their traditions. Nicodemus, despite the traditions of the Pharisees, became a secret follower of Jesus. He defended Jesus before the Sanhedrin (John 7:50) and along with Joseph of Arimathea (also a Pharisee) came to claim the body of Jesus after His crucifixion (John 19:39).

Now that we know the background of this meeting, let's look at their conversation as it was recorded in the book of John:

> 1) Now there was a man of the Pharisees, named Nicodemus, a ruler of the Jews;
> 2) this man came to Him by night, and said to Him, "Rabbi, we know that You have come from God as a teacher; for no one can do these signs that You do unless God is with him."
> 3) Jesus answered and said to him, "Truly, truly, I say to you, unless one is born again, he cannot see the kingdom of God."
> 4) Nicodemus said to Him, "How can a man be born when he is old? He cannot enter a second time into his mother's womb and be born, can he?"
> 5) Jesus answered, "Truly, truly, I say to you, unless one is born of water and the Spirit, he cannot enter into the kingdom of God.
> 6) "That which is born of the flesh is flesh, and that which is born of the Spirit is spirit." (John 3:1-6)

Nicodemus came at night so he would not be seen with Jesus because of the strife between Jesus and the Pharisees. Nicodemus, as a teacher of the law, pays Jesus a compliment by calling Him Rabbi, which means teacher. He states that Jesus is from God because of the signs (wonders, miracles, and healings) He was doing in public. Nicodemus was not expecting what happened next. He had not even asked a question before Jesus makes a statement.

THE KEY WORDS

Jesus already knew what was on Nicodemus's mind when He made His remark: "Truly, truly, I say to you unless one is born again, he cannot see the kingdom of God" (John 3:3). Focusing on the key words in this statement, we will get a fuller meaning of what Jesus is saying. The first key word is "Truly, truly", or "verily, verily" as used in the King James Version. "Truly" comes from the Hebrew word, AMEN (aw-mane'), which means "sure" (free from doubt), "truly" (in accordance with fact), or "so be it"[1]. Jesus used "amen, amen" throughout His teaching whenever He desired to make a point. Jesus is pressing the importance of being born again to Nicodemus by starting His statement this way.

The next key word is "unless", or "except" in the King James, which is translated from the Greek word EANME (eh-an'may) meaning: before, but, except, not, or unless. Further defined[2]:

"Before"	(in front of, in advance, ahead)
"But"	(On the contrary, yet, except, save, unless, if not)
"Except"	(With the exclusion of [all else])
"Not"	(negation)
"Unless"	(except under the circumstances)

Eanme used here refers to "seeing the kingdom of God." Another way of looking at this statement is: "unless, negating all other possibilities, or except under the circumstances of being born again, one cannot see the kingdom of God." This is the only way to see the kingdom of God". Jesus makes it very clear that: "You must be born again." (John 3:7b).

Finally! Look at the words BORN and AGAIN:

BORN: (from the Greek word) GENNAO (ghen-nah'-o), to procreate (properly of the father, but by extension, of the mother); figuratively, to regenerate: -bear, beget, be born, bring forth, conceive, be delivered of gender, make, spring[3].

31

Basically we all understand what born, or being born, means. But, the interesting definition here is the figurative meaning, "to regenerate" (1. To affect a complete moral reform in. 2. To recreate, reconstitute, or make over, especially, in a better form or condition)[4]. We get the impression that Jesus is referring to making one better. We can get a clearer understanding for this in the word AGAIN.

> **AGAIN:** (from the Greek word) ANOTHEN (an'-o-then)," from above"; by analogy, from the first; by implication, anew: - again, from the beginning (very first), the top[5].

The first meaning, from above, is significant. But the analogy of "from the first", and the implication "anew", is more important. The word ANOTHEN is only used in one other place in the Bible. A closer look at that reference will give us understanding of how to best interpret its meaning: "But now that you have come to know God, or rather to be known by God, how is it that you turn back 'again' to the weak and worthless elemental things, to which you desire to be enslaved all over 'again'? (Galatians 4:9). Let's look at a segment of this verse in the King James Version: "...Ye desire again to be in bondage." The implied meaning here is clearly "to return to a former state."

A 1929 FORD

Using the implied meaning of "Born Again" in John 3:3, we can define "Born Again" as "to return to a former, and better state." How does this apply to Man? When a person becomes "Born Again" he returns to the same relationship that Adam had with God. By a crude analogy, it is like restoring a 1929 Ford to its factory-new condition with every original molecule to paint, atom of steel, and even the unworn tires.

HOW LORD?

Nicodemus' reply in the fourth verse was only a natural reaction to Jesus' profound, mind-shaking statement. Nicodemus asked:

"How can a man be born when he is old?' (John 3:4). Nicodemus was most likely an old man and his mother dead. The statement was most unsettling for him. But Jesus explains His statement in verses five and six. Again Jesus starts with: "Truly, truly", then ". . . unless one is born of water and the Spirit, he cannot enter the kingdom of God" (John 3:5).

Verses five and six are important in understanding what "Born Again" really means. The statement "unless one is born of water" is commonly interpreted to mean water baptism. Although water baptism is an essential part of Christian life, it is more probable that Jesus is drawing a parallel between verses five and six. Jesus says in the first part of verse six: "That which is born of the flesh is flesh" (John 3:6). Being "born of water" and being "born of the flesh" is most likely referring to child birth. This is an important point, because physical birth gives a person the right of being able to enter the kingdom of God. If this were not so, then Satan and his fallen angels would be able to be "Born Again", and they would have a second chance to enter heaven. Angels were not born but created in heaven. Unlike man, angels were not created with an independent will. God will not let heaven be troubled by sin again. We are being tested for obedience to God. This is one of the reasons Jesus was born into the world through normal childbirth.

The second half of verses five and six draws a second parallel. Verse 5 says: "and the Spirit," and verse six says, ". . . and that which is born of the Spirit is spirit". These references show a second type of birth, spiritual birth. The capital "S" in spirit means the "Spirit of God" or the "Holy Spirit". The thought here is that something is taking place in the spirit of man through and by the Holy Spirit of God. This change is the recreation of the spirit of each new believer. The new or recreated spirit is from God. The Apostle Paul explained it this way:

> 17) Therefore if any man is in Christ, he is a new creation; the old things passed away; behold, new things have come.
> 18) Now all these things are from God, who reconciled us to Himself through Christ, and gave us the

ministry of reconciliation, (2 Corinthians 5:17 & 18)

RECONCILED TO GOD

Upon being "Born Again" we become reconciled to God or have a "restoration to (the divine) favor"[6]. When this restoration takes place, we have Spirit to spirit communion with God. This can be seen in the outline of the three-part man. A double line illustrates the separation of God and man since the fall of Adam.

#1   **GOD**
==

                          COMMUNION
                               :
(SPIRIT)   **INTUITION**
                               :
                          CONSCIENCE

(SOUL)   **EMOTIONS**   **WILL**   **INTELLECT**
                               :
                          BONE
                               :
(BODY)   **BLOOD**
                               :
                          FLESH

This second outline shows our relationship with God after being "Born Again".

#2   **GOD**

                    COMMUNION
                         :
(SPIRIT)   **INTUITION**
                         :
                    CONSCIENCE

(SOUL) **EMOTIONS**   **WILL**   **INTELLECT**
                         :
                      BONE
                         :
(BODY)   **BLOOD**
                         :
                      FLESH

THE END OF SEPARATION

The double line in the first outline represents the veil or curtain that separated the "Holy Place" from the "Holy of Holies" in the Jewish Temple in Jerusalem. The "Holy of Holies" was the resting place for "the Ark of the Covenant", or "The Mercy Seat of God". The High Priest was the only one allowed to enter the "Holy of Holies". He did this only once a year on the day of "Atonement". At the time Jesus died the veil of the Temple was torn in two from top to bottom:

> 50) And Jesus cried out again with a loud voice, and yielded up His spirit.
> 51) And behold, the veil of the temple was torn in two from the top to bottom, and the earth shook; and the rocks were split, (Matthew 27:50,51)

The tearing of the veil is symbolic of God and man reestablishing their relationship. The veil of the Temple was a symbol of the separation of man from God by Adam's sin.

35

RELATIONSHIP

The "Born Again" man now has a Spirit to spirit relationship or communion with God. This is the same relationship Adam had with God before he was disobedient. I have left the single dashed line in the above outlines to represent a change in the communication between man's soul, or mind, and his spirit.

Man's spirit now knows the difference between good and evil. Through his intuition and conscience he now knows the difference between right and wrong. The fallen man does not have the influence of God. So he listens to the body or external influences. Man still can hear from his spirit, which caused conflict with the external influences. To eliminate the conflict, man stops listening to his spirit. This process occurs over time and is called conscience searing. Man becomes more and more dependent on his emotions and intellect to make decisions.

Once a man becomes "Born Again", he is now influenced by God. But, because man is not familiar with how to listen to his spirit, he does not readily hear what God is saying to him. It takes time and practice to learn to hear one's spirit. People often say they heard God speak to them. In actuality, what they heard was their own spirit relaying what God said through Spirit to spirit communication.

A spirit to spirit communication can happen to non- "Born Again" people. I call this sideways spirit to spirit communication. This is what happens with spirit-mediums when a person develops the ability to hear his spirit. In this type of case the spirit to spirit communications is with an evil spirit.

Another type of spirit to spirit communication is often called Extra Sensory Perception (E. S. P.). This is when a spirit being communicates information. Yet another way is when a person "senses something". They will act on the "feeling" and find a friend or child in a dangerous situation. The last type a Spirit to spirit communication is when the "Holy Spirit of God" speaks to a person to have them accept Jesus as "Lord and Savior". Many of the readers of this book will have this type of experience.

Once a Spirit to spirit relationship is established between God and man, man starts to change. This change comes from within, as God influences a man's spirit, man slowly desires to change. Many times the persons dress, actions, habits, and even personality will change. This is a "transformation", unlike our prison systems that try to "reform" prisoners from without. Reform usually fails because it is against the person's will.

CHAPTER THREE

HOW DO I BECOME BORN AGAIN?

The next question we ask is, "HOW does this happen?" By what means or procedures can a person be "Born Again"? To answer the "HOW", we will break this chapter down into three parts. First we must understand who the man Jesus is. Second, we will come to the understanding of the mechanics, or mechanism. Third, we will learn the procedure, or steps one must take to become "Born Again." To help define the "HOW", we will look at the words "BELIEVE" and "FAITH." Also, we will look at the "LAW" or "LEGAL" reasoning behind all of this.

Most of what we know about Jesus is from the Bible. His birth and the events leading up to His birth are told by two men. The first is Matthew, a tax collector for the Roman Empire and later one of the original twelve Apostles, who wrote the first book of the New Testament. The second man is Luke, a doctor, who became a follower of Jesus after Jesus had returned to heaven. Doctor Luke interviewed people who knew Jesus, then he wrote the third book of the New Testament known as Luke.

GOD SAVED!

The first thing we need to know is what the name "Jesus Christ" means. Jesus is English for the Greek word Iesous (pronounced ee-ay-sooce'), and the Hebrew word Joshua. Joshua means "Jehovah saved". Jehovah is the Hebrew word for God. Jesus' name literally means "God saved." Christ is not Jesus' last name. In the culture of the time there were no last names. The practice was to use the father's name. Jesus would have been known as Joshua ben Joseph in Hebrew. The "ben" means "son of", so the translation is, "Jesus the son of Joseph".

The word Christ is the English version of the Greek word Christos. Christos has the same meaning as the Hebrew word Messiah. These two words mean "anointed". To anoint someone was to give that person power and authority. This was generally done by pouring oil over the heads of the kings and priests of that time. The anointing of Jewish kings and priests was believed to have been accompanied by the presence of the Holy Spirit of God. Jesus is called the Christ or the Messiah because He was anointed by God. This is recorded in all the Gospels. Matthew tells the story this way:

> 16) And after being baptized, Jesus went up immediately from the water; and behold, the heavens were opened, and He saw the Spirit of God descending as a dove, and coming upon Him,
>
> 17) and behold, a voice out of the heavens, saying, "This is My Beloved Son, in whom I am well-pleased." (Matthew 3:16,17)

This event can be considered Jesus' coronation because the Holy Spirit of God came upon Him. It was from this point on that Jesus' ministry began in earnest. This makes Jesus the Anointed One of God who reigns with power and authority as the King of kings and Lord of lords.

THE VIRGIN BIRTH

The birth of Jesus is extremely important to our becoming Born

Again. The virgin birth in significant as to whom Jesus is and why we can be reconciled to God. First we need to look at Matthew's account of the birth:

> 18) Now the birth of Jesus Christ was as follows. When His mother Mary had been betrothed to Joseph, before they came together she was found to be with child by the Holy Spirit.
> 19) And Joseph her husband, being a righteous man, and not wanting to disgrace her, desired to put her away secretly.
> 20) But when he had considered this, behold, an angel of the Lord appeared to him in a dream, saying, "Joseph, son of David, do not be afraid to take Mary as your wife; for that which has been conceived in her is of the Holy Spirit.
> 21) "And she will bear a Son; and you shall call His name Jesus, for it is He who will save His people from their sins."
> 22) Now all this took place that what was spoken by the Lord through the prophet might be fulfilled, saying,
> 23) "BEHOLD, THE VIRGIN SHALL BE WITH CHILD, AND SHALL BEAR A SON, AND THEY SHALL CALL HIS NAME IMMANUEL," (Isaiah 7:14) which translated means, "GOD WITH US."
> 24) And Joseph arose from his sleep, and did as the angel of the Lord commanded him, and took her as his wife,
> 25) and kept her a virgin until she gave birth to a Son: and he called His name Jesus. (Matthew 1:18-25)

Verse 18 states that Mary is betrothed to Joseph. A betrothal is an engagement contract. The only way Joseph could get out of the betrothal would be to divorce Mary. Under the old Jewish law, because she was pregnant, Joseph could have had her stoned to death because of her apparent infidelity. But instead, Joseph went ahead and married Mary and he refrained from having sex with her until after Jesus was born.

Verse 23 shows a prophecy of Isaiah made 700 years before the birth of Jesus. This prophecy was well known and every young Jewish virgin was believing to be the chosen one to bear the Messiah. The supernatural fertilizing of Mary's egg also fulfilled a prophecy made by God. We saw this in Genesis chapter three during the fall of man when God said to Satan: "And I will put enmity between you and the woman, and between your seed and her seed; He shall bruise you on the head, and you shall bruise him on the heel." (Genesis 3:15). The seed God referred to is the supernaturally fertilized egg of Mary. Remembering the three-part man, we can understand that the eternal spirit in that egg is the Spirit of God, in the form of Jesus, the Son of God.

The fact that no natural father is involved, means that the sin nature of man is not passed on to Jesus. But the natural birth of Jesus gives Him the right as a man to enter the kingdom of God. Recently scientists have come to the conclusion that all the blood of a child comes from the father. Besides Jesus not having the sin nature of man, He had the very blood of God in Him.

DO NOT MARVEL

Jesus continues teaching Nicodemus:

> 7) "do not marvel that I said to you, 'You must be born again.'
> 8) " the wind blows where it wishes and you hear the sound of it, but do not know where it comes from and where it is going; so is everyone who is born of the Spirit."
> 9) Nicodemus answered and said to Him, "How can these things be?"
> 10) Jesus answered and said to him, "Are you the teacher of Israel, and do not understand these things?
> 11) "Truly, truly, I say to you, we speak that which we know, and bear witness of that which we have

seen; and you do not receive our witness.

12) If I told you earthly things and you do not believe, how shall you believe if I tell you heavenly things?

13) "And no one has ascended into heaven, but He who descended from heaven, even the Son of Man.

14) "And as Moses lifted up the serpent in the wilderness, even so must the Son of Man be lifted up;

15) that whoever believe may in Him have eternal life.

16) "For God so loved the world, that He gave His only begotten Son, that whoever believes in Him should not perish, but have eternal life.

17) "For God did not send the Son into the world to judge the world, but that the world should be saved through Him.

18) "He who believes in Him is not judged; he who does not believe has been judged already, because he has not believed in the name of the only begotten Son of God.

19) "And this is the judgement, that the light is come into the world, and men loved the darkness rather than the light; for their deeds were evil.

20) "For everyone who does evil hates the light, and does not come to the light, lest his deeds should be exposed.

21) "But he who practices the truth comes to the light, that his deeds may be manifested as having been wrought in God." (John 3:1-21)

Nicodemus, in verse nine asked, "How can these things be?". Jesus had already said in verse seven, "Do not marvel that I said to you, 'You must be born again'". Jesus, in verse ten, possibly a little frustrated with Nicodemus, answers back, ". . . Are you the teacher of Israel, and do not understand these things?". Nicodemus had spent his whole life studying the Law and the Prophets (what we call the Old Testament), and he does not understand what Jesus is telling him. The story of the Messiah was foretold throughout the history of Israel in the sacred writings. Jesus is expecting an educated man of Israel to understand what He is teaching.

In verses 11 and 12 Jesus goes on by saying:

> 11) "Truly, truly, I say to you, we speak that which we know, and bear witness of that which we have seen; and you do not receive our witness.
> 12) If I told you earthly things and you do not believe, how shall you believe if I tell you heavenly things? (John 3:11,12)

It is quite plain that Jesus was telling Nicodemus to shape up. Jesus had talked about ordinary things, and Nicodemus did not understand. How then can he comprehend heavenly things. Earlier, in verse eight, Jesus had given Nicodemus some idea of heavenly things by using the wind as an analogy: " the wind blows where it wishes and you hear the sound of it, but do not know where it comes from and where it is going; so is everyone who is born of the Spirit." (John 3:8). First, remember that Nicodemus did not have a modern scientific explanation of the wind. Jesus was likening the wind to the Spirit. We know that the wind is there, but we do not see it. We can feel and see the effects of the wind, but we cannot see where it comes from or where it goes. It is true of the Spirit. When we become Born Again, we feel and perceive the effects of the Spirit, but we cannot comprehend where the Spirit comes from or where it is going.

SON OF GOD/SON OF MAN

Jesus, in verse 13, establishes His deity by saying, "And no one has ascended into heaven, but He (Jesus) who descended from heaven, even the Son of Man." (John 3:13). Jesus will be the first to return to heaven. This is an important fact that we will discuss later. The term "Son of Man" is used throughout the four gospels: Matthew, Mark, Luke, and John. This shows Jesus' natural human side, His right to be on earth, and His right to later enter heaven.

Son of Man is in contrast to Son of God, which shows Jesus eternal nature, or His God nature.

Verse 14 refers to an event that happened over twelve hundred years before. Nicodemus was familiar with the story of the fiery serpents.

> 6) And the LORD sent fiery serpents among the people and they bit the people, so that many people of Israel died.
> 7) So the people came to Moses and said, "We have sinned, because we have spoken against the LORD and you; intercede with the LORD, that He may remove the serpents from us." And Moses interceded for the people.
> 8) Then the LORD said to Moses, "Make a fiery serpent, and set it on a standard; and it shall come about, that everyone who is bitten, when he looks at it, he shall live."
> 9) And Moses made a bronze serpent and set it on the standard; and it came about, that if a serpent bit any man, when he looked to the bronze serpent, he lived. (Numbers 21:6-9)

Jesus makes a comparison in verse 14 between the image of the fiery serpent and the fact that He would be lifted up on the cross. "And as Moses lifted up the serpent in the wilderness, even so must the Son of Man be lifted up;" (John 3:14). This comparison is the first strong indication in this conversation that Jesus is to be crucified. Jesus here is showing how man can be Born Again. When the children of Israel were in the desert and a person was bitten by the serpent, all he had to do to be healed was to look at the serpent on the staff. Likewise man must look to Jesus, the Son of God, to be healed of his sinfulness (or disobedience).

THE MECHANICS

Jesus shows us the mechanics of being Born Again: "For God

so loved the world, that He gave His only begotten Son, that whoever believes in Him should not perish, but have eternal life." (John 3:16). The first key word here is "believes":

> **BELIEVES:** (from the Greek word) PISTEUO (pist-yoo'-o), to have faith (in, upon, or with respect to, a person or thing, i.e., credit); by implication to entrust (especially one's spiritual well-being to Christ): -believe(r), commit (to trust), put in trust with.[7]

We are to believe or to have faith in Jesus. Faith is part of the mechanics of becoming Born Again. We must have faith. What is faith and how do we get it?

> **FAITH:** (from the Greek word) PISTIS (pis'-tis), persuasion, i.e., credence, moral conviction (of religious truth, or the truthfulness of God or a religious teacher), especially reliance upon Christ for salvation; abstract(ly), constancy in such profession; by extension the system of religious (Gospel) truth itself:-assurance, belief, believe, faith, fidelity.[8]

Chapter one showed how God tested Adam to see if he would be obedient. Adam failed the test and was cut off from God. Adam was thrown out of the garden. But, God had a plan to change man's fallen state. God's plan was a second test to give each man a chance to show his obedience to Himself. The Apostle Paul in his letter to the Romans tells us that we all have been given a measure of faith so we can choose to believe that Jesus is the Son of God: "as God has allotted to each a measure of faith" (Romans 12:3b). We must take the measure of faith God has given us and use it to believe that: God is, that Jesus is, ". . . His only begotten Son," (John 3:16), and that ". . . Jesus as Lord, [and] . . . that God raised Him from the dead," (Romans 10:9).

THE LAW REQUIRES PUNISHMENT

The other part of the mechanism to become Born Again is the fulfillment of the law. God's law requires punishment when it is transgressed. When the angels were found to be disobedient, they were removed from the presence of God and condemned to hell for eternity.

God established the law through Moses. This is referred to as the Mosaic Law or the Torah, found in the first five books of the Old Testament, also called the Pentateuch. The Mosaic Law is divided into three parts, the civil, moral, and ceremonial laws.

The civil law in the Torah is the same as any other body of laws. The moral law deals with relationships with each other. Many civil laws incorporate many of the moral laws in them, such as rape, incest, and other sex-related laws. The ceremonial laws are the unique laws of the Torah. This body of laws covers the sacrifice of the lambs, rams, bulls, and other animals. These sacrifices come under many names, but in general they are called sin offerings. In Old Testament times, the shedding of blood was required to cover sin. Animals were used in place of man, who was the real law breaker. These types of sacrifices were at best temporary. A permanent solution was needed. So, in God's plan, He sent Jesus to be the final sacrifice for all sin.

To be able to fulfill the law and the need for a pure and holy sacrifice, Jesus had to be pure and holy, spotless, without blemish, and perfect. He had to fulfill all 613 of the individual laws of the Torah. Jesus did this by first being born of a virgin (an undefiled woman). The seed of the woman was supernaturally fertilized by God, so He (Jesus) is God, thereby being perfect and holy. Jesus then lived as a man, facing all the same temptations of a natural man. Remembering the three-part man, Jesus has the body of a man, but His spirit is God. His fulfilling of the Mosaic Law made Him the only one who could be sacrificed—shedding His blood (the blood of God), taking away the sins (or disobedience) of all mankind. Jesus is: ". . . the Lamb of God who takes away the sin of the world!" (John 1:29). Jesus replaces the animal sacrifices of the old law or the Torah, because He is both God and Man.

THE LAW SATISFIED

Jesus makes this plain: "For God did not send the Son into the world to judge the world, but that the world should be saved through Him" (John 3:17). Jesus fulfilled the law; He became the second man or surrogate. The apostle Paul in his letter to the Romans said it this way: "For as through the one man's [Adam's] disobedience the many were made sinners, even so through the obedience of the One [Jesus fulfilling the 613 laws] the many will be made righteous" (Romans 5:19).

One thing that must be understood is, that Jesus actually died a spiritual death on the cross. This was the first time that Jesus was separated from God. We see this during the crucifixion of Jesus: "And about the ninth hour Jesus cried out with a loud voice, saying, "Eli, Eli lama sabachthani?" that is, "My God, My God, why hast Thou forsaken Me?" (Matthew 27:46). Without a spiritual death Jesus could not die physically and would have had to have been rescued by the angels of heaven. Jesus paid the price for the sins of all mankind by this act of spiritual death. The best definition of "righteous or righteousness" comes from Dr. William Kaiser, former director of the Word of Faith Leadership and Bible Institute in Dallas, Texas: "To be in right standing or have a right-standing relationship with God." We can only be put into a right-standing relationship with God because of Jesus' dual nature as both God and Man, and because He perfectly fulfilled the law.

THE PROCEDURE

Next is the procedure or the steps involved in becoming Born Again. The answer again lies in the Apostle Paul's letter to the Romans in the tenth chapter:

> 8) "But what does it say? "THE WORD IS NEAR YOU, IN YOUR MOUTH AND IN YOUR HEART" 9-that is, the word of faith which we are preaching,
> 9) That if you confess with your mouth Jesus as

Lord, and believe in your heart that God raised Him from the dead, you shall be saved;

10) for with the heart man believes, resulting in righteousness, and with the mouth he confesses, resulting in salvation.

11) For the Scripture says, "WHOEVER BELIEVES IN HIM WILL NOT BE DISAPPOINTED."[10]

12) For there is no distinction between Jew and Greek; for the same Lord is Lord of all, abounding in riches for all who call upon Him;

13) for "WHOEVER WILL CALL UPON THE NAME OF THE LORD WILL BE SAVED."[11] (Romans 10:8-13)

The first step is to ask Jesus into your heart making Him both Lord and Savior. Then you need to confess that Jesus is Lord, and believe in your heart that God raised Him from the dead. This seems too simple to be true! Man always looks for a complex solution. Have you ever watched children playing a game? At first the rules of the game are simple, but as problems arise more rules are added. The final results of this are the rule books for every major sport in the world. But God's ways are not man's ways. God keeps it simple. Like the original test that God posed for Adam, the test we face is just as simple. We simply must confess that Jesus, the Son of God, is Lord, and believe in our hearts that God raised Jesus from the dead.

IT'S SIMPLE!

Simple, yes, but God made the test so simple that even a child can have understanding of how to be Born Again. God's desire is that all should pass the test. "The Lord is not slow about His promise, as some count slowness, but is patient toward you, not wishing for any to perish but for all to come to repentance," (2 Peter 3:9). God never intended for man to go to hell. He had to make the test as simple as possible so even the simplest person could understand and pass.

Repentance is another important part of being "Born Again". To repent, simply means to turn around 180 degrees, turning away from destruction and turning toward God: "He who believes in Him is not judged; he who does not believe has been judged already, because he has not believed in the name of the only begotten Son of God." (John 3:18). Jesus states it this way: "Truly, truly, I say to you, he who hears My word, and believes Him who sent Me, has eternal life, and does not come into judgment, but has passed out of death into life." (John 5:24). Part of repentance is to make a confession of our sins or disobedience to God. This is part of the cleansing process. Repenting is the turning toward God, and the confessing starts us on our way from death to life.

How does one become Born Again? In a conversation between Nicodemus and Jesus, Jesus makes a most remarkable statement: "...unless one is born again, he cannot see the kingdom of God." (John 3:3b). To enter the kingdom of God we must be born of flesh and we must be born of the Spirit. Being born of flesh sets us apart from the angels. We see Jesus' dual nature of being both God and man. Jesus came from a woman's seed which was supernaturally fertilized. It is only through the seed of a woman that Jesus is brought into the world to destroy the power of Satan. This fulfills God's word as recorded in Genesis:

> "And I will put enmity
> Between you and the woman,
> And between your seed and her seed;
> He shall bruise you on the head,
> And you shall bruise him on the heel.
> (Genesis 3:15)

THE ONLY ONE

Remember from chapter one that bruising of the head is symbolic of a loss of power and authority. The bruising of the heel is symbolic of Jesus being crucified on the cross. The crucifixion of Jesus was the sacrifice necessary to fulfill the law. Jesus was the only one able to be sacrificed because He was the only one who was both God and man. Also, He fulfilled all 613 laws. We are all given a measure of FAITH so we can BELIEVE that Jesus is Lord, and that God raised Him from the dead. It is necessary for us to confess this and to confess that we are sinners or that we have been disobedient to God. God desires that not one of us should go to eternal destruction, but that all will accept Jesus as His Son.

CHAPTER FOUR

WHEN SHOULD I BECOME BORN AGAIN?

In light of what has already been said in the first three chapters, "WHEN" to become Born Again would seem to be academic. I will explore the aspects of time, death, the decision, heaven, the spirit and the soul. This seems to be an impossible task, but I feel the reader needs to look at these elements (although in brief) to better understand the nature of being Born Again, and "WHEN" to become Born Again.

Let's look first at "WHEN" you should become Born Again, or at what time you should make a decision to give your life to Jesus Christ. Some may think that ideally the best time to be Born Again is just before you die. So then you can eat, drink and be merry in the mean time.

LET'S DREAM FOR A MINUTE

Here is an analogy that may help clear up some of the aspects of being Born Again. Let's dream for a minute. A messenger comes to you and tells you that a very rich person has arranged for you to live in paradise for the rest of your life. A paradise that has everything you could ever want or desire. Where there are no snow storms, hurricanes, floods, insects, or any other inconveniences. But, there are some strings attached. You must pick up your airline ticket and be ready to leave on a certain day and time. The messenger warns that if you do not pick up the ticket and be at the airport on time, the ticket is void and not transferable or refundable. Now, who would not run right out to the ticket agency and pick up the ticket, if for no other reason than to see if what the messenger told you was true.

The time of departure in this analogy is the time we will die. The trip is death and paradise is heaven. The rich person is Jesus Christ and His messenger is a pastor, evangelist, or the author of a book about being Born Again. Unlike the airline we do not know the day nor the hour we will die. The most uncertain thing in life is our time of death. If we knew the time we would die, we most certainly would get our ticket to heaven. Death can come at any moment: driving home in our car, a heart attack, an airplane crash, or a gunman at a fast-food restaurant or a school. Death can come so suddenly that we do not even have a chance to utter a word.

THE GREAT HALL OF LIFE

Life is a great hall with two doors. The door we enter by is called birth, the door we exit by is called death. While we are in the great hall of life, we move steadily toward the door marked death. During this time we have an opportunity to make the most important decision of our life. We can accept God's way, confessing Jesus as Lord and believing in our hearts that God raised Him from the dead, or we can reject God's way. After we pass through the door called death, we are instantly lifted heavenward or fall downward into hell.

Continually, I have presented the three-part man. Looking again at the outline of the three-part man we see the spirit; soul or mind; and the flesh, blood, and bone body of man:

COMMUNION

:

(SPIRIT)   **INTUITION**

:

CONSCIENCE

:

(SOUL)   **EMOTIONS**   **WILL**   **INTELLECT**

==

BONE

:

(BODY)   **BLOOD**

:

FLESH

The double-dashed line represents death. When we die our spirit and soul are separated from our body. The apostle James said it this way: "For just as the body without the spirit is dead, so also faith without works is dead" (James 2:26). Adam's body was formed out of the dust of the ground, then God breathed in the breath of life (SPIRIT), he became a living being (SOUL): "Then the LORD God formed man of dust from the ground, and breathed into his nostrils the breath of life; and man became a living being". (Genesis 2:7). The spirit is the essence of life. The spirit is unquenchable, it does not die or pass out of existence. Our spirit is that part of us that is made in the image and likeness of God:

> 26) Then God said, "Let Us make man in Our image, according to Our likeness; and let them rule over the fish of the sea and over the birds of the sky and over the cattle and over all the earth, and over every creeping thing that creeps on the earth."
> 27) And God created man in His own image, in the image of God He created him; male and female He created them." (Genesis 1:26,27)

OUR EARTH SUIT

Our spirit is the real us. Our bodies are only a type of protective covering we need to live here on earth. We can liken our body to a space suit. A space suit has no life in itself, but becomes alive when the astronaut gets inside of it. The space suit is only needed so the astronaut can live in outer space. Once the astronaut is finished with his suit, he takes it off and goes on living as before. So it is with us. Our body is an earth suit, in itself there is no life. But when the spirit enters, the spirit gives the body life. When our body physically dies, we leave it and go on to our final reward. Remember that our bodies were extruded from the dust of the ground: "The LORD God formed man of dust from the ground, and breathed into his nostrils the breath of life; and man became a living being," (Genesis 2:7). After our spirit leaves the body, the body returns to dust: "By the sweat of your face you shall eat bread, till you return to the ground, because from it you were taken; for you are dust, and to dust you shall return." (Genesis 3:19). Or "then the dust will return to the earth as it was, and the spirit will return to God who gave it." (Ecclesiastes 12:7).

Ecclesiastes 12:7 shows the separation of the body from the spirit. The body returns to dust as we saw in Genesis 3:19, but the spirit returns to God for the purpose of being dispatched to heaven or hell. John 3:18 shows us that until we accept God's way we are already judged: "He who believes in Him is not judged; he who does not believe has been judged already, because he has not believed in the name of the only begotten Son of God. (John 3:18). The moment of death seals our destiny forever. Our course is set for either heaven or hell. The Apostle Paul in his letter to the Romans said it this way: "For the wages of sin is death, but the free gift of God is eternal life in Christ Jesus our Lord." (Romans 6:23). Based on whether we have accepted or rejected Jesus as Lord and Savior, we receive a reward of death or the gift of life.

FIRST CLASS TICKET TO HELL

Man is born into the world dead to God. If he dies before being

Born Again, he is eternally dead. Borrowing a term from computers, the default mode of being born is to be born with a first class ticket to hell. In 1996 a group of boys brutally raped, tortured and killed a girl to ensure that they would go to hell. They destroyed a precious life and wasted their time because they were already guaranteed of going to hell.

Some have said that heaven will be boring and they would prefer to go to hell. I am giving my impression of what hell will be like for those who go there. Imagine being strapped into a pair of boots that are bolted to the floor. You can never get out of the boots. Then gasoline is poured onto the floor and ignited. Because you are a spirit you will never burn up, but you will feel the burning of the gasoline. Of course this is only an impression, but the sensation is real. This is because a spirit without a body or God is in intolerable pain. Some fun!

So! When is the best time to be Born Again? "But", you may say, "I am not worthy of being in the presence of God", and you are right. Not one of us deserves to enter the kingdom of God. Again the Apostle Paul in his letter to the Romans said: "for all have sinned and fall short of the glory of God" (Romans 3:23). Not one of us is worthy on our own merit to come into the presence of God. We are born with a sin nature and in need of a Savior. Jesus came into the world to both fulfill the law and to be sacrificed to pay for our offenses. There is a very good explanation of why it was done this way. We see this in the Apostle Paul's letter to the Church at Ephesus:

> 8) For by grace you have been saved through faith.
> And that not of yourselves, it is the gift of God;
> 9) not as a result of works, that no one should boast.
> (Ephesians 2:8,9)

We are eternally indebted to God and to Jesus Christ for our salvation. I said in chapter one that God would never let heaven suffer violence again. We, being indebted to God, will give Him our eternal gratitude and allegiance. We will not give our allegiance begrudgingly, but out of a loving and thankful heart for all that God has done for us. We receive our salvation by grace through faith. Grace in this respect means something that God willingly gives us that we do not deserve, the unmerited (unearned) favor of God. At the end of Ephesians 2:8, we see salvation as a "gift." A gift is a present that is given because the giver wants to give it out of love. A gift comes with no strings attached except that we accept the gift given. Who on Christmas morning would leave a valuable gift under the tree unopened? But that is what we do if we do not accept the gift from God that was bought at a great price . . . the crucifixion of Jesus on the cross.

Here is one more thing about the gift of salvation. We have had our idea distorted as to receiving gifts. Who as a child has not, in the excitement of Christmas, done something he should not have done. Then, Mom and Dad come and say, "If you are not good, you will not get anything for Christmas." We associate our being good with our worthiness to receive a gift. This is a reward for being good and not a gift. A true gift is given not because we earned the gift, but because the giver wanted to give the gift. So, not one of us is worthy of the gift of salvation. God has given us this great gift because He wants none of us to go to eternal destruction, and because of His love for each and every one of us. "But", you say, "you do not know what I have done. Surely God cannot forgive me of the terrible things I have done." Are you greater than God that you can out sin His grace, mercy, and love? There is nothing that cannot be forgiven! Even Hitler, if he had sincerely called on the name of Jesus in the moments before he died, would have been saved.

WHEN? NOW?

When is the best time to become Born Again? "But", you ask, "what benefit is there to becoming Born Again?" The first benefit is the obvious one, you will pass out of judgement and receive the promise of spending eternity in heaven. "But, I may not like it in heaven?" We know so little about what heaven will really be like. Some have said that heaven will be boring. But remember that we are spirit beings and our spirit was made (designed) to live in heaven.

When we get to heaven, it will be a "deja vu", like we were there before. It will be as natural and as comfortable as putting on an old pair of slippers. Heaven will feel like we have finally come home.

So, again, when is the best time to become Born Again? Well, there in no time like the present. Right now? Yes! Right now is the best time, wherever you are; at home, at work, in an airplane, or just lying on the beach. The shepherd-king, David, said this in Psalms:

> 7) Where can I go from your Spirit? Where can I flee from your presence?
> 8) If I go up to the heavens, you are there; if I make my bed in the depths, you are there.
> 9) If I rise on the wings of the dawn, if I settle on the far side of the sea,
> 10) even there your hand will guide me, you right hand will hold me fast.
> 11) If I say, "Surely the darkness will hide me and the light become night around me,"
> 12) even the darkness will not be dark to you; the night will shine like the day, for darkness is as light to you.
> 13) For you created my inmost being; you knit me together in my mother's womb. (Psalm 139:7-13 N.I.V)

MAKING A 180

God is wherever you are and waiting for you to turn to Him. He cannot come to you until you turn to Him. The word "repent" means to change your mind, to turn around. To repent is make a 180 degree turn from the way you are going and turn to God. This is done through a simple prayer. Prayer is speaking to God and you do not need to use "thee's" and "thou's." Simply talk to God as you would talk to your best friend. It does not matter who or what you are - a prostitute, a homosexual, a murderer, an adulterer, an abortionist, a drug addict, an alcoholic or anything that is wrong in the sight of God - **God loves you so much that He sent Jesus to die**

on the cross to pay the price so you can be SET FREE!

Simply pray these words to God, asking Jesus into your heart. You will be saved (Born Again), and you will receive eternal life in heaven.

**"O God in Heaven,
I believe that Jesus is Your Son.
I believe You raised Jesus from the dead!
Jesus, come into my heart.
I receive you now as my Lord and Savior,
I repent of my past sins,
And I am looking to you for my future.
Fill me to overflowing with Your precious Holy Spirit. I receive you now, Jesus! Amen"!**

THE RIGHT TO HEAVEN

If you prayed this prayer, believing that Jesus is now Lord and Savior of your life, you are a Born Again Christian. You now inherit all the blessings and promises of God. I said in chapter three that we are like Adam when we are Born Again. This is true because we are now in spiritual communion with God as Adam was. Now, we are even better than Adam was. Adam only had the promise of heaven. But, Adam failed the test. We, as Born Again Christians, possess the right to heaven. We are now joint heirs with Jesus. We are members of the family of God. We have become a totally new creation. Our spirit is now in communion with God and ready to enter heaven.

When we are physically born, it is a beginning. Likewise, when we are Born Again, it is a beginning. Being Born Again is not just an event, but like birth itself, it too is the start of a new life. The way you grow is to be fed. The food of the spirit is reading the Bible, praying, going to church, and to have fellowship with other believers. We are to grow and mature from an infant to an adult. When we are Born Again, we mature from our old nature to a new nature, the nature of God. There is a controversy over, if someone is Born

Again, are they always Born Again. The Apostle Paul wrote this to the church at Rome:

> 38) For I am convinced that neither death, nor life, nor angels, nor principalities, nor things present, nor things to come, nor powers,
> 39) nor height, nor depth, nor any other created thing, shall be able to separate us from the love of God, which is in Christ Jesus our Lord. (Romans 8:38,39)

I believe there is one condition that can separate us from God. We can make a willful decision, just like the willful decision to become Born Again. We can decide to turn away from God. If we do make such a decision, we can never come back. (Mark 3:28,29). So, do as the apostle said in his first letter to the Church in Corinth; "Do you not know that those who run in a race all run, but only one receives the prize? Run in such a way that you may win." (I Corinthians 9:24). A runner only can win the prize if he runs the full race. We must do the same. We must run to the end of the race to ensure that we win the prize.

And always REMEMBER:

GOD LOVES YOU

AND

JESUS DIED FOR YOU!

Notes

1. Strong's Exhaustive Concordance of the Bible, James Strong, Dugan Publishers, Inc., Gordonsville, Tn 38563

2. Ibid.

3. Ibid.

4. The Random House Dictionary of the English Language, College Edition, 1968.

5. Strong's Exhaustive Concordance of the Bible, James Strong, Dugan Publishers, Inc., Gordonville, Tn. 38563

6. Ibid.

7. Ibid.

8. Ibid.

9. Deuteronomy 30:14

10. Isaiah 28:16

11. Joel 2:32

Your Notes

Printed in the United States
19070LVS00001B/280-300